M

AND OTHER POEMS

M

AND OTHER POEMS

JOHN PECK

Evanston, Illinois

TriQuarterly Books
Northwestern University Press
Evanston, Illinois 60208-4210

Printed in the United States of America

ISBN 0-8101-5055-7 (cloth)
ISBN 0-8101-5056-5 (paper)

Library of Congress Cataloging-in-Publication Data

Peck, John, 1941–
M and other poems / John Peck.
p. cm.
ISBN 0-8101-5055-7 (cloth : alk. paper). — ISBN 0-8101-5056-5 (paper : alk. paper)
I. Title.
PS3566.E247M3 1996
811'.54—dc20 96-24855
CIP

The paper used in this publication meets the minimum requirements of the American National Standard for Information Sciences—Permanence of Paper for Printed Library Materials, ANSI Z39.48-1984.

For Ingrid

For visible humanity is in many respects also not human. . . . Therefore, although each person is human in one sense, there are many senses in which each is not humanity.

—Proclus on Plato's *Parmenides*

The soul must lead itself to execution.

—Eckhart

CONTENTS

NOTES AND ACKNOWLEDGMENTS

"Anasazi," Navajo for "ancient enemies," and rendered by anthropologists as "the old ones," were the original dwellers in the Four Corners region of the American southwest from the twelfth through the fourteenth centuries. The phrase *vestigium pedis*, which supplies me with the title for another poem, once stood as a reminder that existential forms point beyond themselves. The radio broadcast mentioned in *"Igitur, Itaque, Dunque, Donc"* occurred in Vienna in 1991.

Work on some of these poems was furthered by support from the Ingram-Merrill Foundation. I offer grateful acknowledgment to the editors of the following journals, in which several of the poems first appeared: *Agni, Amicus, The Notre Dame Review, The Paris Review, PN Review.*

WOODS BURIAL

At the rapids father and boy pitch in a young birch
        laid out by winter.

It is the March of mud roads and triggered hearts.
   That boy leaps as the limber corpse
   hurtles a chute, his father chuckles.

If they really knew what history is,
even though they're in it up to their necks,
they'd feel it, the tug, the cold tilt. They'd stand, shiver.

But how much smarter is that? And how am I better?
     It is that log I've got to be,
        shot straight, unstuck from the banks,
sluicing my wood-lice through the white gates,
            hurling home.

AUTUMN SYLLABICS ON THEMES FROM HORACE AND THE CHINESE MASTERS

Efficiency in the great round
moves darkly to completion: circling
though not returning. Its curves disperse
winds and carve bone. And yet any seized
fullness easing through grace to release
surges from springs, no tributary.
Between asperity and sweetness
gushes one water with two tastes. So

broach the hoarded wine and commit pace
to the powers, their timing,
                                        achieve
    what remains by yielding what
    has already been taken
    though not given up. And much
    will be given, though not much
    in seeming, so be now
a taker, with your friend give over
    at last what can never work.

    Boughs slough their white loads and swing
into spare curves, the crow landing there
    scans bluish drifts for little
    footprints, one hunger gazing
after others, one velocity
    subsuming the rest: the deer
drifting up defiles, the goatwalker
    of gone and coming summers
        gazing towards the peaks.

SO THE NAME OF THAT PLACE WAS TABERAH

because the fire of the Lord burned among them
—Numbers 11

Past Gary, to Chicago on the train,
stench from the slaugherhouses streaming east,
black bascules yawning above acid, the brain's
imbalances like yeast
tilting, spreading the hidden face of rain

in a vast scrawl along the miles-wide front,
scaling the whole expressive inventory:
lust from morning skillets for darkness to blunt,
sadness out of the story
of simple meat, sudden wars and long want,

bacon hanging in the grandparents' pantry
and thrummings of a power station at night—
biography eclipsed in the black chantry
of childhood, and second sight
in slag with its magma suns under looming gantries.

NIGHT-BLOOMING CEREUS

Democracy of effort,
then aristocracy of poise
achieved, both mount this cruel
crest of blossom bobbing
past a day's sheen
to court attention and cajole joys.

One would have to have
those eyes, wing-ferried, facet-frizzed,
of the visitor, or lover,
or plunderer, or master
enslaved, the dragon
as fly, to see it for all it is.

So this one says it plainly,
not with our lisp of angel's ape:
I am that flesh of body
kept awake by spirit
into the far hours,
I keep on burning, I escape.

Innocence that we lose
in the embrace of such contraries
is well lost. But we trade it
along our sole stem, not
through Life upper-case
but *a* life, for the trade it carries.

For the gray grit of it.
For chromed arch misting a storm's rip.
For trinkets dulling the edge,

and unifying sweat
down spine and brow,
cooling on kidney, eyelid, lip.

My eyes anticipate
the night watches, that I might think
hard on the unthinkable.
But sensuous is this fiber
of the climb, sway,
and flowering, clayey is the brink.

Carries the whole hell-bent
on high and breathes the heights low-borne—
and what my rank is matters
not very much where such
strangeness reaches
and sap of light floods both ways torn.

ANASAZI, ANCIENT ENEMIES

I rubbed wax crayon against blowing paper.
From the rock face footed a dancer white through red.
  My family gave me over
  to it, gone for the river.

Were I a peasant harvesting grapes near Beaune
in the last century, even, I might have dreamed
  a saint lifting off for Arles,
  Les Saintes Maries de la Mer,

and knowing about cannon in that long peace,
might have been troubled therefore that my flier
  hauled a magnum of the best
  and bloodied the west sky with it

and vanished. My fisting that loose sheet in place
was secretarial, not visionary!
  Already in that decade
  small tribes entered the void

like windows on a skyscraper when the bent
janitor makes his way. But those flick back on
  each night, costly difference.
  It is not only portents

in dream or flapping images of the gone
or the soon-to-be-going or the tremblingly poised
  that catch like undertow
  the foot in tide-rip toeing

down the singing or remembered beach.
We study populations in the forests,
  we hold the paper flat,
  mark, note, warn—the dictated

prophecies do their work, we do some work—
cut horn from rhinos so they won't be poached.
  But, to go on from there,
  one needs to stand in the doorway

some evening and feel the air as if it were fire
pulling illusionlessly, letting the draw
  of one fact heat its chain
  of links, such as, Japan

clear-cutting forests in Siberia
where tigers not already harvested
  lope their dwindling range,
  two hundred as the hinge

for their growled arc of existence, bones of the others
ground to powders for old men's potencies.
  One needs to feel the tug
  of the draft on skin, the drag

of process utterly anciently itself.
Faster, now, the pull is from birth through dwelling through
  dissolution, along lines
  streaming through us, ageless winds.

GETTING AT WHAT HAPPENS

There was a wife named Hope, who reconstructed every
stanza her husband, whizzed by the raven, could not inscribe.

Tarnish among tall gildings in the Hall of Mirrors
sinks from infiltrating sun, parquetry crackles.

Sleek carter of first fire, Apollo from Louis's fountain,
aims horsepower at plate glass cooled before the revolutions.

Losses at hand, with lined faces, what have they
to do with the grassy palace, the dwindling and combed prospects?

Doctors pulled at the splinter
of fat in her Homeric heart, but she sang the days.

If one sways with it faithfully, the pendulum
takes back what it etched with dribbled sand. The sun also.

What they talked about in the cities, what they heard
their hearts fractioning, forecasting, was not all that happened.

A carpenter, planing and sanding,
stands and unstiffens, then hears them: mice in the rafters.

They talked about what they thought revolved inside them,
and what they thought had bitterly happened to them. And talked.

There was a wife named Luna, who had to reverse her tiara
whenever light filled it, annulling her fine entrance.

The old year, crone on the back of a Vézelay yeoman,
tends goose girls in the tale, her gift is love's beginning.

Joinery combs grainy solids, toothing them, to bend planes
seamlessly, then shut them fast. Where ends the beginning?

Ah but then blood happens, unstoppably, and so
why, then, a filmy stream of counter-gleams?

Room roofed over, stanza struck and ringing, meet in
the dancer's live arm, torsions of grazed pasture, forest.

Filthy hunters through them chase throat sound with horn sound,
hugged couples in the high grasses press closure to genesis.

Lancehead corroding there to dark bread, plough and tractor
tipping it forth, guards with damp sachet the queen's bedchamber.

And so the joints lock: sadness somewhere in it but finished,
its polish smells of hair and the gilded flooring of brooks.

And begins to press past even closeness, wing not the raven's
but hers who remembers, a mind past the hours, throbbing both ways.

WINE OF THE SOLITARIES

Resonance in the hated process
and the despised figure, are we prepared
to hear its hum across our cherished
assumptions, and violate our course?
And so hear the new beauty in the perished?

Core amore viso riso gente innocente—
chimes at midday, shadowless, nonetheless
bang at obdurately daylit certainties
with harmonies past the obvious, they rain down
the rebuke of hard-won clarities:

in the first stanza, that bright room
of the canto addressed to his wife,
Leopardi rhymes love with heart, smile
with face, and people with innocence,
but it is like the flash of a file

in those miniature armies we have lost
with the ground beneath them, in our tilt
into the indiscriminate, all clawing
together in one slide. Like a file
catching sun gleam, then, while drawing

chinking out of the infantry square
to extend its front rank and broaden
around the opponent and wrap him in,
folding over his flanks with that long
cutting edge, backed by the rest, to win

the center at day's spookiest hour,
unshadowed apex—so that with this
brave extension of his quick means
the strategist across that fulcrum
insures that this night tureens

of soup gladdened by slaughter will pour
to his companies while in his own tent
after the officers have taken leave
he will decant the saved wine from skins
of his own goats, no one to receive

the downward narrowing of red light
within the glass's stem, that treasure
hauled in fur across the white passes,
save him alone. Turning it, his hand
finds the gleam steady, amasses

all that he brings to it fluidly
after the clanged wager and its throw
from his hand through hands not his own.
Neither blood nor victor's mantle that sheen,
nor ode's ripple, but a thing known

only from the solitude of his
stewardship in the fields, his villa
the baked focus of his gaze. And we,
massed beyond all this in the blue,
populous and impossible, at last see

the contraries escape us to enter
his seasonal efforts with the hacked vine,
battle's counter-rhyme trimmed with other steel,
as ancient as marriage, as the bed canopied
within, his arched vein at her heel.

LITTLE FUGUE

An apple paring
curled from the knife wetly
down my thumb—
and what I had failed
to do rightly touching that life
next to mine, wearing
late afternoon's numb
luminosity, impaled me.

A hunter knee-deep
in salt marsh, whom Anton Chekov
might have set there and then left,
back to doctoring,
or choked off as too dark, wanton,
met the steep
flailing of teal, trailed their shrill lift,
but stood only, hearing them.

Pouring the last tea
of an evening, dark amber
alive, breathing in quintessence
of India,
I felt limber bark
sheathing the shrub of my life's tree
with root good, but dense,
dark, local, raw there,

and so in dark he woke,
the seeing doctor, two simple
profiles of linked characters
in his air,

cruel, good, a pair ample, true
across that split yoke,
true to its splayed force—
simple so rare, though.

OCCAM'S RAZOR PLEDGES NO HOSTAGES TO FORTUNE

Predication is routinely outpaced by the ache of process.
Thus, possession's claim falls short, but thus too
the wholehearted outwaits all erosions to spring
in a spatter of the unexpected. Hid glories hang
unmanifest in pig iron puddled in bulbed Bessemers,
in the turned stomach subsiding and sacks lugging anthracite.
Predication! Skeptics peak early, disemboweling discourse.
Idealists secrete one late pearl and take fire in the gate's shadow.
Hara-kiri fascinates then saddens, but pale primroses
distend themselves at dusk to drink in night, lanky lamps.
The old historian staying at his desk through the uprising,
his young housekeeper, unenamored, climbing stairs with tea.
Seneca was eloquent as he entered the hot bath with
razor,
his wife after him, oratory rises over the spreading stain,
its accomplishment of coda is not to be underrated, it is *la gloire*
as the rose is, lemony spreadings of the implicate
transposing through bobbing auras the aroma
of what steps forth and then reclines like the clay couples
at their nestled banquet suspended on tomb lid.
But such is not the deed. That lay seeded long since
to drift scent through phases following, in the small hours.

MONUMENT

Wrong turn, then on rounding a night-wide lake
pink trotting feet, swerve, thump, weasel or badger:
time will suddenly differ, bent reed break,

or warbler, not across a royal hall
window to window dark to dark but veering
from guardrails just when I slowed, into the grille—

this is the edge of the entire machine
and I am back of it with my two hands,
turn wand floating beneath the dials' lit brain—

there is a condition, an atmosphere,
much as vacancy waiting for something like form
to fill it, that eludes impact, that's not here

yet was here a moment ago, the way tiny
people on parapets, or trudging with cattle
under low clouds, meeting the blind spot go grainy,

or turning back for a squirrel in the Val Bregel
she found it no longer twitching but laid flat
where young Giacometti through a trill

of vapor saw a walker narrow in
like the Etruscan figurines and pierce
luminous space it had filled, take bronze, and lean.

ATTIC CANZONETTA

At mute distance, farther
than a poised lance's leap,
the disc of some reflector,
face of metal asleep
to itself in raining sun,
catches the darting, furtive
or brash face of someone
who stays unaware, assertively
gazing yet blind because seen
by the unnoticed. The heaped
fire of space, the detector,
shines like his emptying,
until he fills it up.
And his is the image it grips
in fulfillment. Witness? There is none.
But images are not gathers
of emptiness. Oh the gap
I must close with this living
across which I cannot lean
with my seeing—oh this giving
always onto it, further!

Heart sets a labyrinth
around the gliding blood,
as if one looped a length
of rope over itself
in a great eight and bound
that graph of the eternal
to the labors of an elf
at the hot juncture. Round
it is, seemingly whole,

yet side by side it is half
itself in rhythmic strength
unknowing. Understood
is the symmetry, yet blind
the feeling of it. But good
comes of the chase, pulling
myself past myself,
if I flood with it. Fatal
for the prince, then, to swing around
in his run and thrust aside
the curtain, glimpsing his fiend
running past along the plinth.

For that cannot be courage
towards the hidden thing,
that is the gleaming edge
of phantasm, changing
while steadily in place.
Paradox speeds up light
till depth works in the surface.
And gleamingly deep is night.
  So argument strives with the gleam
of argument! And mirrored
though they run they lift one hum
from the blurred sun floating inside—
fire-flakes along our streams
of jabber and hymn are the sound
sun makes, seen with unseen—
I saw you once, light into light,
veiled fire alive and at large!
Slowly, with the weight
of a Greek worker turning
his ponderous dance, I am learning
how to explore the space
I inhabit: staring at

my feet as they lift up worlds,
gingerly heaving a great
whirling from verge to verge
of balance, I reach out
to nothing more than my limit
and nothing less. It floats furled
about me, its speed is blinding
yet no mirror, and I sing its image.

SOUNDLESS TUNE IN THE JEWEL

Horrors as underbelly to winning this
    human life, its treasure my master.
    This, then—but not its bazaar,
horror and chintz, styrene and alabaster.

Heaped along the bridge's ledges, crammed shops
    smeared muddy in Arno, Firenze!
    Stops for the trinkets at war
in wishing's cubbied darks, curbing flow's frenzy.

Not them, but neither the chorus at Delphi, a smother
    of clangs around a widow
    mother, her mind ajar
over the fife-led drums. Yet water shadow,

and one crossing beneath toothed towers and flags . . .
    memory stirs, turns a wheel,
    sags with the banners, lifts far:
revealed, the rare is plain yet something sealed

floating soundlessly, no bridge for that—
    revealed yet anciently clear there.
    That, then: transparent bar
in the crystal within the wave on wave breaking nearer.

FIRST THINGS

Powers, in dispossession,
repossessing their birthright past disaster!

What I am after, the original of it,
is not at the peaks, nor washed in valley rivers.

It mingles with the refugees in a camp
over from Tibet in Punjab, it takes a chair

where lamas studying
lunar eclipses with a bright blue globe
stay after class with flashlights and pencils to giggle,
rolling shadows over continents.

And leave. It stays in the corner, unobserved,
inherits the pine smell of desks, and the sweat smell,
and the sound of wind from the passes,
and enters sleep with eyes open.

VESTIGIUM PEDIS

As rain across a lake's face
chills it, leaving streaks of warm runoff
and rising current darkishly vital,
just so one day they shine clear,
mottlings across skin, spotty streaks
waiting to be bannered by flaws
of wind drifting the pocking water.
That day points to the footprint, the vestige:
dearness of revealed patterns harbored.
Yet though I trailed this shore down
into evening then back up past dawn,
finding the same litter, toy shovel,
cigarette pack, and the brave cairns,
it is one kingfisher squat on his boulder
exploding through the shower, razoring
the other shore with his black crest,
that flashes to me the mirror's spin:
discipline of all disciplines, not to
supply past likenesses for the fact rising.

HANGING FIGURES

I'd worked my way through half her trays,
cards from all Italy,
and found the poet who took on Apollo
hung from his wrists, Marsyas,
and turned to pay for him, to see
her wracked shoulders and blurry
face and wet hands and tried to follow
the words through tears, *Signore,*
mi scusa! whereupon I began to sing
the formulae, the god's tuned durable things.

He thought, *October blue and gold—*
that's how it runs, he thought,
an old widower fresh in his shock.
But his grief wrote it. Amber
Frost was what he'd thought he got,
staying him in his need,
Nothing Gold Can Stay his rock,
so Frost was what he tried to read
at the memorial. But I most remember
his own blurted line that gray November.

Having traipsed to Bern in the rain
to get things by Nezval,
haunting ditties he wrote in the war,
I couldn't know I'd gain
the face of a Czech that would stay when all
the poems had receded:
gilt titles glinting around a door
behind him as he rose and pleaded,
Mais il était collaborateur! the breath
of the transposed illuminated by wrath.

Rome's midnight bus pours me downhill
to the train through guts, betrayal,
empty and leaning through the curves,
when the tall drunk sways over
to the exit, making his avowal,
I was a pilot twelve years!
then asking my name and waving: *Nerve,*
you've got it too, I can tell! Disappears.
Italian, with flawless English, weary plover
blown from his perch, somewhere else to recover.

FRÈRE JACQUES, FRÈRE ANTOINE

At a bus stop in Arles a fellow wounded in the Last War
winced into sunlight: *Oui, they are beating the drums against*
les juifs again, and the Moors. France is an old man!
An old pink thing lacking one eye, with his good one he gazed
through and past me to something which held his interest
and at which, after a silence not uncomfortable, he smiled.
Were I to tell this to acquaintances they would brand him senile.

Below a ridge in the Drôme, a goatherd huddled in mists.
His little carboniferous eyes glinted. He was not clean.
A kid bucked and sprang. I asked him how long a goat lives.
He stared, shrugged, and up the slope of wonder intoned,
Who knows?
          I asked how many in his herd, and discussed income.
I started to turn over figures in my alien mind, doing
sums and multiples on his eighty head, with calvings pyramiding
upward through geometric promise. He watched me.
He knew what I was thinking, and what I was going to propose.
Monsieur, he chuckled, *NO one needs more than eighty goats!*
And were I to relate this to the literati, they'd call it anecdote.

MEDITATION IN THE MIDST OF ACTION

It was a clear day on a full street, with
  everything for sale.

A white-hair stood by his frozen cascade of pins,
  medals for shock troops of labor,
  brooches from power stations,
five years had thrown him clear of that collapse,
  bronze horseman and bright hammers.

  This from Petersburg also,
    'Fortress of Peter' it says,
  and there rounding from blues
of young night bent a woman drawing water
in her gold bowl towards her gold flesh, N Y M P H A .

  Medea watched them also,
sword dangling—servants filling tureens
that spill along their skirts, cord over cord,
ropes of it bound me once to that low relief
  in a long hall of gazing,

long because with everyone of an age
I'd been thrown clear. Children that were not hers. . . .
The children. Not thinned and fenced, and not burned.
Metal when stroked in a reflective way
  gives water, a flowing stillness.

But cool through din and clang, rash acts, displacements.

If only we could drink it, it would cure us.

POLYBIUS

As with historians out of the Great War
for whom diligence failed to fulfill their call,
I've had to sense, no spiritual warrior,
that being out on cliffs it is not all,

or even half, to gauge the lean into wind,
to balance in it and still claim the ledge,
although that may be much, the knife's point skinned
to one crystal, grief parting down the edge.

More than much. But not enough for strange life,
long thrust unnamed. The name, staring, inherits
a stone gate with false door, high cenotaph,
dark polish showing flights as submerged spirits.

Rebirth! That I climbed to the Capitol
out of the vanquished heights perfects the pattern:
the clank of the law, its close fit in seeming full,
pays its due to the void caw of the bittern.

But the life climbing and the tearing air,
it might have been among the peaks of Chungnan,
always came to full quiet, to the pair,
one old one older, in their emptying dawn:

What is coming will shatter the categories.
So, as for your ambition, you'll be learning
it will do you no good. Mist rifting firs,
and down on the river's bend a barge turning.

ON TINY OBSIDIAN BLADES FROM PEARY LAND, GREENLAND

No farther east, none,
nor stayed they for months or weeks:
through blackness the eye's light
chipped these, scattering black flakes,

half a finger's length
but with a tension that flings
from Bering Strait through
full north to extreme dawnings,

into the nooks most
barren and coldest to us,
star-shorn nights, and so
past even the disastrous.

Failure no measure,
they compress under some weight
not quite destiny's
because not reduced by fate,

but made small by sparse
possibilities of such
grander cohesions,
the driven hunt's trove and trash.

And are still useful:
no weeping at some image
on a screen, no fate
loved emptily, such roughage.

These, at the full stretch
of hare-tracking and fox-chase,
meet philosophy's
shattered mirror and lost face,

breath on the still air,
shrinking into the litter
of pursuit, under
day-years and the wind's glitter.

Harsh miniatures!
The light most ancient, clear,
is of forgetting,
of memory without fear

and without content,
cutting no flesh, horizon
looking to the rise
of a disc long since risen

where one can drop free
of you, refound talismans
of identity,
beyond fortune and past plan.

What you are will stay
in the mind that flares, passes,
the strewn ledge, the site,
with its ice plow, its mosses.

ROMANZA

The untutored Richter showed us, but now there is this
bent girl. It is the middle of the long Andante.
The sufferer has penetrated her suffering,
not figuratively but really. One has to want to,
with the ancestors, and the race also, gathering.
She has convened them, the sign of which, hint to
radar watchers, is the shine of runoff trickling
from her hump. Its rock, concentrating into
quartzes, will show on their scanners as a searing
dot strengthening to core whiteness among scanty
blues repeating across sands of the swept ring.
She has found that part of Provence or Burgundy
in which honored ghosts abandoned a sunk dwelling,
and has poised herself on the chalk doorsill, twenty
horses champing within her thighs, and has cleared that rung
into, not space, not landscape, but their minty
lavendery cloud-mongering sandstone-levering
bed of forcings in the backmost band of mind, plenty
nor scarcity categories there, but emergence, ringing,
her elbows maintaining elevation while flinty
shoulders mass over wrists

from which everything
whatever its modes pours with cobalt coherence, chanty
or chorus. But there is no naming it now, only following.
She has found the chink, she has gotten through once
with the entire kit on her back, no slackening
of present actuality, its freight, and where that chance
has been taken it can be taken again, untrembling.
She has not protected herself with what the art wants
usually to shelter, nor has she done duty by fleeing
what the art in its deepening narrowness demands.

A sweaty cave has turned out into heart's shattering.
Gone landforms into future beachheads, the homelands.
Future? The rarely present, the abiding there unfolding.

IGITUR, ITAQUE, DUNQUE, DONC

Because the orb goes on
turning, because sliding waters
among themselves lend turn
to the drift of
all driftings
here in this sphere
of all spheres,
there comes
spin cumulative, lateral, momentous
swinging the axis of each microcurrent:
the electron if interrogated replies
digitally, but with a
flick of the wrist
also, *I remember! I was there!*
longitude latitude and azimuth
degree of inclination, with the factor
of a just-calculable, half-drugged rotation
away from formerly, dear doric home
my ballast tanks remind me,
my anti-roll tanks
also, therefore I have queered the tie ropes
ever so slightly from the assaulted wheelhouse
to the moon-battered rudder, thus: hold her
steady as she goes, but not quite; and *her*
is in a manner of speaking a pretty
liberty, swerve, note for the sake of grace
antiquated yet ineradicable,
the tongue rolls with it upward
on the long-skewing swells.
Because
of what they do to cracked pack ice

whose playing fields roll and sail *coriolis*
like gleaming fighters from their formations or plates
of the continents gooselike into green haze
through the eras, there are certain effects,
therefore, to wit: Herr Wagner
  billeted in the foc'sle
plowing into peaks in a lacy gown
while scoring the saga of a naive Fool,
is swung ever so slightly around to starboard
into the grip of Hagen's nephews in belted
  brown shirts; therefore, to wit:
Herr Doktor Professor Jung is heard prophesying
long since his passing through a Norn's tremolo
on Austrian radio. Therefore! to wit,
  to woo:
          the maker is
consumed, not by acids of seamy regard
but *in the course of things,* which is law passed
in chilly deeps and in the currents veering
past velvet cheeks of land masses; is consumed
by an undeflectable turning, *ad versus.*
Therefore the practice of Glenn Gould when he trembled
stranded on his floe, which I've been startled
to recognize in my own doings, stands
not as the hermit's measure only but
also as countermeasure. He would drive
to a big truck stop, sit at center table,
and listen: bass clarinet against horn,
violin inquiring oboe narrating,
until he could take up, thread, separate
  the phrases, time their entries,
model their crests and cadences, so turning
that flow which is there undreaming of itself
corrosive with heats and colds swirled nourishing slimes
crystalline saline torsions of exchange

knotting and unraveling in the sun and blind,
into his worthy partner, less than fate
and more than folly, and conductable,
entering what he could strictly feel and handle
before he stuffed those hands in pockets and shuffled
across a drifted lake into glared north.

TOMBEAU FOR VERNON WATKINS

Awash in grass and oak leaves calmed and then shivered,
a face of woman, or man, Chinese, or Danish,
mask set by when the play, or the actor, wavered,
its leather peaty. Treasure steeps in that tarnish!

Heroine and hero, bearers-through,
driven imaginer behind them dreaming,
have dwindled. Where I stand, though ancient, a few
moments reveal as shorespreads of the streaming

boundary, patience beside their lappings reveals
body behind, lost-vast, at ease in mind,
and in those features shuckings of the seals,
with love light-sundered gone for the dark to grow kind.

TRIO THREADED ON LINES FROM THE PARTHIAN HYMNS

Grasp happiness with this leavetaking!

Wet strew from sycamores
shot my boot out towards the bend of Tiber
when I was halfway down
stone risers to the embankment's mulled gibber,

quietest lappings, and toss
of trash, rufflings of dusk-muffled gulls,
like muted strings for the stripes
squiggled from lamps down the depth's gliding pulls,

all this registering
in the swift tilt of the world away, rolled gap,
as my head sought its hard pillow
and my frame slithered through that stair's loose grip.

How much quieter there:
overhead, on all sides, the withdrawn traffic.
Farther, the slide of dark cloud.
Dank smells, no annals, no lights. Cold flow prolific.

Long before I learned
that Pasolini dropped to the same view here,
stunned, I looked up at it,
two meters thin, history's glitter and fear.

Buonarotti's bridge,
Cocles's clicking sword, the litter of bills
from American cars on the night
of the elections: up there, on the seven hills.

As in a kiva's hub
a gully lets the dancer burrow down
under a trap and fling it
flagrantly back and shoot out as god, clown,

and with his anomaly
focus the plane he returns to, so, with fury,
jackanapes, go on up,
with innocence the blow has restored, go, harry!

you were jailed in the roaring void
and dragged captive over every threshold,

Into dens of approbation
in the dun north
was ushered the anomalous
disturber and refiner, desolation's
allegorist who drove forth
from his south the ripe figures, scandalous—

vitalities as victims, throttled
or trumped, or married
whitely to mortuary meats,
himself the stainer of youth, fabled mottled
stingwing to the staid virtures, ferried
for brief honoraria to the sweet seats.

The villa with dusky screening room.
To the book signing.
The watering hole of the prize-givers.
To the seminar. Assiduously bright gloom.
He entertained their questions. Dining
quickly, he abandoned them, the long livers,

he enplaned once again for hell,
   and entered standing,
ambassador of the pierced boys,
of men who although sold out would not sell
something of a countermanding
fantasy, nourished against increasing noise,

and stupor of empty liberties,
   and garbage stenches
in their own streets, and the tiredness
everywhere, most at the heart of hot energies,
most even in the loins and haunches
of consolation, wearied out to weirdness.

And there a few of the servitors
   bashed in his skull
and shattered his hand and ruptured his heart with the wheels
of his own car, where Tiber snores
out to vastness, where the legendary null
of Hades began once, and now bright mist steals.

you orbited through the whirl of births,
you were pillaged in all the cities.

   Pastorals have flown
out with the probe, or in, down the cell's helix.
   Zero trajectory,
or else picnickers in the Mendelian calyx.

Between, I stretch a giddy cable.
   Towards you I balance,
Persephonēia, you said you'd return,
and so my left hand I shall let wobble
as reason, my right as dalliance,
between the infinities a rhythm to learn.

Pastoral has dissolved
as tea swirls from leaf shred into hot ichor.
Towards you I lean and climb,
refugee in red gown, brave with the seasons' liquor.

Flown and dissolved, while the rampart spreads.
Perhaps a neglected
fountain burbles yet in the garden,
the weedy center. But certainly the dead
shall live, out on the unprotected
wind sag of the wire, on, where you hum them pardon.

VIATICUM

Up under waterfalls,
passing the lacquer workers over their bowls,
the air for them cleaner there
but some still going insane,
a walker towards the Alps from a lake's brief plain
took the route of the peddlers, their stacked wares.

Tin funnels, gingham bolts.
Toffees, tobaccos, spices, nails, augers, felts.
Lace for the rare body shift.
Sweated grace of exchange
above the passes, where no armies range,
where herb is heal-all but footing is no gift.

I catch it: the drift down years
backward, slipping, as if I blur the fear
that mounts in the peoples yet hovers,
that smears haze even through valleys
shadowed by the blown peaks. With the bellies
of serpents I must feel this, not eyes of lovers—

that what is thus feared is failed
for going ungreeted, or for being impaled
with a warlock's dug-up corpse,
crucifix over a stake
in the high pines. That with its old tread it will take
its winding climb through the levels that dusk absorbs.

FOR A SMALL CHORUS

The tightest square is mere event's. Around it
repetitive cities, hazed microcircuits, pile and jam,
until the pressure within it makes
vacant lots, deserts,
and chines of stripped peaks whisper of their fellowship
in moods of many hearts,
down chines of the ventricles.
To whom assign the blame? The altar stands unbuilt.
Ushered away from that spot
where touch crumbles, as naive
urchins get pushed from the opera, all deities.
To draftees held in departure barracks by khaki police,
five at each door, pistols drawn,
and files under guard chinking
towards transports gleaming in night,
blessings from a father
who neither scars nor devours,
yet touches: blessings from some hand!

By some Dravidian river, under bankside groves bending,
beside waters rifted with cloud, by shores untracked,
the body of giant humanity
mounded and decked,
soaked with berry, draped with plantain, branch-boned,
lies out under day's sweep
while beside it a stage
disposes actors in regalia of the gods and devils,
miniature gestures
of men and women their score.
And like a huddle of preschoolers beyond that shape,
the watching generations time sceneries of truth.

Near one of the interior rivers
it stands clear, shines out
in cloth and bangles, voice drift
volleying over dust.
It steps forth. And animals
watch from verges of forest.

AVE

Not quite the god who lies back in milk's ocean
out of whose reveries curdle the worlds, not, then,
like island hands breaching then sleekly gone;

nor yet an orant from the catacombs,
linen her seamless length, her rosy palms
lifting a semaphore in the tiered tombs;

though somewhat these. More like seeing hands
of the support dancer reaching up, not tense
to be filled, yet filled before the other lands,

or on a Munich ivory Peter's hands
at the back (while forward Thomas's grope the wounds)—
floating, starting to curve like window blinds

reefed gently as their puller takes in day,
they pause along their rise, foresails one ply
of paleness across the glow, fluttery,

or shining like the palms of the Elgonyi
wet with spit to greet breaklight, ebony
leathery from the hunt, or the grainy

handprints of a painter held at attention
among herd animals and through commotions
of the chase down a rockface, or Asian

palms of an Eskimo into sunrise
after he has puffed on them, and across glaze
greets that day as long as a season. Like these

rather than a crook's dropping his gun,
or spookball from another planet, or thin
stalker cornered, hands up in unison

within a folktale flooding through little eyes
    from page or screen, the gaze
    passivity's or fury's

down each miniature fate holding it:
those all swim in and out, anticipate
dear phony real life minute after minute—

but when in the tub a girl rolls the sheen of atolls
from her wrists, or his arms float under swells
as brother in the hot soak beside candles

their father has set on the enamel rim
slowly lifts a hand and watches steam
banner off in the half-dark, there is some

earliest opening breathing, Vishnu with Peter
bracketing it, the hunters, too, in utter
balance. And she is quiet. And he knows better

than to say anything, think anything
as the heroes disappear, as their gleaming
colors go. Something far older there, smoothing.

FROM THE HEADLAND AT CUMAE

People expected that the evil would finally drain away.
—Aleksander Wat, *My Century*

Faded and baked here to a tawny grit,
spills of blood and seed from humanity
called from it for its crimes against mute earth
gully in footpaths, dribble down to the sea,
payment now and forever drawn from birth
through flesh's sunny darkness. Light yeasts in it.

And if I find the slope to crumbled temples
of that light's god dragging at me through heat,
shallow degrees of slant up to remnant stone,
then something more than burnt air, or the repeat
of weight known as time, pulls heavily in this zone,
something the bone brings, terrible though simple.

Phoibos, slayer at distances with shock,
sower of plague and arrower of healing,
tension of bright-dark beyond spanning, love
will not quite cast out evil while revealing
your fissionables. The raven was your dove.
Heavy isotopes hum with crickets in rock.

Neither woman nor man, my driver laughed
when his lights torched writhings down the far shoulder,
cross-dresser in the night beyond Naples, huge,
sinuous, crooning as we shot past. Life seems older
in its variant forms, drawn by the centrifuge
to the rim and swinging, swayed in time's dream uncalfed.

For the vast thrower, shafter of quivering force,
sex was filigree in whoever served.
Pythoness, yes, wombed keeper of those coils
in the wet cellar where tongue darted and swerved.
But her own throat when it swelled with voice knew toils
past a man's strength, torqued bulging from the source.

And that young man fitted with bone and thong
and membrane from his withers by his father
the maze molder, when he climbed into flame
itself in the high nucleus, dripped as slather
down the sky's maw. Union there, with an aim
at the center, crisped on a central soundless gong,

sizzling from his overreach extended
back on itself and down, the soundless hurry
of the sea far below minutely riven,
trembling in place, diamonds in blue slurry
nowhere disturbed yet flecking everywhere, driven—
all this a boy's cry endlessly thin, suspended.

The sybil when at last her throat disgorged
its burdens rumbled like a pawing bull,
or the bull-fiend on Krete, and shrilly warbled.
Birds ride the bull's hump in stone graphs, that full
barbarity at poise piercing now the garbled
clang of Ikaros, over us tensile and forged.

This in the crumpling whistle of shells and frags
in their close arc. Philosophy gets precise
when it turns practical. This in our background whir.
Archimedes, old Fermi in your eyes,
naked, ecstatic with theorems that assure
conclusion, your city falls, your hacked flesh sags.

There was a sprig which, if you bore it in hand
on landing here, your pilot drowned and your herald
crushed in the surf, would bend and seem to listen—
there was a branch that trailed her voice through imperiled
corridors to throats of the dead, and glistened,
then brought you back to your breath near shining sand.

And there was pelt from the solar scavenger,
its blond mane tossing with your workings, turning
catastrophe to triumph, lion crud
strewn now on waves, coat of the charger burning
obsidian cobalt platinum and mud
in craters of the shaker and avenger.

Eroded skull of this squat promontory,
nubbled shrine over cave by surf hypnotized
before deeps enameled with fire's mosaic,
you are the structure lucid though pulverized
behind the logics, and the omens prosaic
in their spelling out, and the blaze of story.

Give me your light! I am the darkened thing
seeking it. Give me your fire and your cry!
But hood me from sulfurs she inhaled when she twisted
over the fissures, give me your hand from the sky
we have fallen into. Give, yes, what you insisted
she utter, rasped uncoilings of your spring!

And then release me to the animal
shy of speech yet steady in ecstasies,
your cousin the outsider's gaze through life,
the drink of it down, and finally mind as frieze
eternally in metamorphic strife
released, sea stone and cloud infinitely small.

And there the migrant and his wanderers
may find the new land, and their future wars
may roll, exhausted in hissing foam, to sink
over the fish spines, and the blunderers
of fulfillment stare at samsaric wink
of ocean, stare and find sleep that dissolves the curse.

MEMORANDUM

I have begun this many times and shall not finish,
nonetheless! Hsuan-tang rendered into our tongue
the sutras he lugged across
ice ridges from India,
and coaxed forth a pagoda
in the capital's lower quarter of sunrise
to shield them from storm and fire.

Those who passed their exams
brushed their names in the arches
that surveyed empire unblinkingly
from four high outlooks.

Along these curving registries of ambition
visitors saw geese climbing into autumn.

Also he had been ordered to set down
a record of his travels, which became
an era's hangout, lovable
master-tattle, all-fathering novel,
anything that any mind found scrutable.
Whereas his sutras lay out schemas
of the orb onlookers peer into
but do not see through: all-mind.
The one world as one mind. And then?

Following their ordeal, during a good decade
examinees took up assignments in every
reach of the bureaus, each more remunerative
than that posting in Philosophy to the lycée
at Le Puy for fledgling Simone Weil.

Through-sight lifts from the sill, webs tucking under,
it leaves insight safe there. Only it
goes on out. Visitors began to call this temple
Pagoda of the Great Goose.

The ninth-month flocks trailing
their navigators aim
at the sun, however obliquely, as in those Vedas
lisping orientation towards Le Puy
eras before Gautama spilled like Caesar
from his mother's side.

Madame Professeur took her pupils past the babble
of the agora, into the Platonic abysm, then turned them
to face the acetylene torch of Pythagoras
and the fusion-orb of Parmenides afloat in night.

It is the human privilege to hang a gleaming
necklace of labored fashioning, *kosmos,* around
the neck of the universe, and wait for compliments.
Unvarying shiver of onset, rolling shifts of glissade:
    pine wind and fire wind.

Tu Fu inscribed his name under the arch coping
                                                                                then
fashioned a quatrain about gosling-diplomates
streaming off towards day's furnace door
and screaming, *Where will I rest?*

        All this by way of reminding you:
we must promote implementations,
rephase the proposals but stay on schedule,
but dump the tapes from their bunkers, shoot
no more bullets ferrying Bach past Arcturus.

Most of the signatures are gone,
only pomposities from the snot-nosed
Ch'ing great-grandfathers of the reborn revolution
hang on above the spring peonies.

How old, those aromas? That is perhaps
not the most penetrating question.

My own recommendation: become arrow, meet the bow,
requisition platinum for the thumb ring,
but snare this with roundabout nets, rely only
    on collateral agencies.

Where the mind perhaps opens
past where mind has definitively stopped,
there hovers the next proposal, the pulsing chinook.

To the code team: scratch contingency plans
for restitutions, scotch all apocalypses.
For they creep back into the galvanics
of fresh feeling, they twitch there. We have ignored the fire
before any judgment, prior to undoings, its coals present.

Read the unwritten and inhale.
Climb to the four outlooks, graduate to dawn's flare.
Sleep not. Still the heart. Study.

RELAY OCTETS

✸

If sound, then why not the full reach of mind,
and if that cantilever then why not the whole
keyboard with its totality of partials?
But then one meets the dragon, pipes up a bright
disciple, *whose two dramas, lieber Meister,*
are suicide and the founding of the state.
My name is a household word, writes the hid teacher
to his ambitious aspirant, *in my own household.*

✸

Three, three, and two, the comeliest proportions
in twice four, carols a bobolink at midtree,
the golden sections of sight flap nostalgic for sound.
But of touch there is no ratio, there are only
gradient, ascent, compression, easing,
and space evacuated, not yearning; filled.
Therefore, Belovèd, middle is neither midmost
nor at the squeezed core, but where breath resumes.

✸

A man who had killed in order to save life,
and had left his clan to guide the foreigner,
never went home. Or, home was what he came to.
The girl who knew that something before and after,
of which no one spoke, was always brimming now,
came to his corner, knitted, did not speak.
What had striven in him and was seeding in her
gazed out over the harbor, through white sails crossing.

✷

Simply because temple and trave rise framed
like verse of the Silver Age, it's not dreaming back
to loop out with those curves on sunflower faces—
points on their net, widening, hold tight
in casts of fishermen, fowlers, and high buds
leafing stone along the load-bearing wall.
Lighthouse beacon sweeps over, that arm bends,
star swirl releasing the torch to a dark cycle.

✷

The beginning of the third Razumovsky quartet
sets one in midstream doubt, amberish dam
for joy's spillover: true beginning starts late.
Slaying the interlopers, he has only just
told her he must go off again, she accepts,
neither climax nor close is the end in their lightning.
And the shaft of it shearing down, it is steadily
here, and the clamor in it is calm, its roar a vast silence.

M

A Poem in Ten Chapters and One Thousand Lines

Avec reconnaissance après une maladie, et pour Sainte Jehanne

Nature has kept everything in view,
the end no less than the beginning
or the intermediate period of duration;
much as a boy who throws a ball in the air.

—Marcus Aurelius, *Meditations* VII.20

I

May have towered above the battle, the mind of that girl,
but where she had taken it now even Chiron could not say.
Was I apprenticed to thronged dreads, the absences
hugged by my teachers? Nature hath mind, though hidden.
I stepped down terraces under compulsion, the slime on them
a milky sheath over pythons, down beveled leg-deep risers.
A scruffy-capped man stepped out, cord over one shoulder
as in guide service among the peaks. A Gascon.
With pursed lips and gesture right he led through a door.
Past it, enduring stars. In my hands a rope, moving.
Knobbly acanthus leaves as on columns at Karnak
vibrated along it against my surprised palms.
As on forty-five-degree slopes tufted beneath summits,
where spruces start straight out and then angle up
to gain the plumbline ordained by day's fire—just as there
each trunk begins as a knee rounded full at the rail,
so each acanthus curved out from the fast green cable.
And as trees at that altitude when thrown by wind
topple not down but back, their roots sheathed and cones
still budding, pliant and roseate, so each leaf flap
sprang to the humming bole shining as it went.
This much was returning, then: inmost spruce of Egypt.
Under such glades in early summer haying begins
on slopes almost as steep, the wide-bed red tractors
dragging spreaders twirling like the legs of flies.
And through my hands from that swift force the tinglings
of pristine growth, twirling through deep space to fall
in nests and tepees on the razed field, prickled and calmed.
Deep: though it was clear that no rope could reach
the latitude of that sun without long since vanishing,
nonetheless, like a high-tension line glinting
over a pass, it curved around the left hip of fire.
Space: though it was obvious that things at such remove

were not to be scanned close up, yet the gases curling
into the corona, a vast iris, were dressed flat
by tugs of a loom's comb, into a strange gaze
which compelled mine to hold it though I fought back tears.

This must be one thread of what you call viriditas.
I faced the fighting abbess, the discriminator
of herbal transformers green from the blurred seasons.
For a warp forming from blackness had cowled itself
over the iron singing reed of Rhein's Bingen.
Whenever feather-tailed barbs shot from her sure lip
duke and prelate learned to duck, a helm's gleam
framing her, for like the merchant's son from Assisi
she had a rider in her, and a yen to ride.
Milk's rise had diffused through her, leaving no one
outlet and no single port. Her answer broke, leaping.
Yes! And the pride of woman and a man's glory
must meet. But my hurt meets the coming wound of Arthur,
woven lay and lament, wound of the next age.
She above her rider, a bit on him too, turned him towards
galactic scatter. What may have glowed over his eyes,
what may have broken like embers over hers, shifted
off and away, communing only where fire rebegins.
As for space, you live among blind conjurers who declare
that the four arrows of the plane and the two of height
turn widdershins in Tibet and on the atolls, unreadable
although crystalline to the insurers of glass towers.
But you sensed it: they are sons of the thaumaturge
who drew the ten thousand strings of the intelligibles
into his hands

at Jena, looking past Bonaparte and Christ
into mirrors, dragging it all close, sinking in
crashing. The ant's fragrant intellect, the bee's quadrille,
the bluebottle's geodesic eye, the whale's pressure gauge,
and the radar of swallows cross-haired on Capistrano

filigreed themselves among her syllables.
Trickles under snowpack and runnels warmed on a beach
burble in the same mode as they make for their source,
breasted phallused black-white streaming twi-sided voice.
A mountain goat's severed forefoot on snowslope
without effort or protection points the way.
Hegel had arced his compass across the whole, whereas
she now vanished into all things, while that sun rested
on living coils funneling down to a void point
or aperture into fullness: window shut onto green speed.

Yes, to be sure, there was the Gascon, *This way, Monsieur,*
on ahead, his quarrier's cap salted with limestone.
And the unreleasable cord towards that orange globe
on its green cone. And where flame seated in that coil
a cushion of hot metal flared outward, petaled
and unsplashing, thinning to gold as if hammered.
This turned counter-clockwise while the cone spun with time
towards its low root. Across the fireball's face
eddies mated, disengaged, redissolved.
Much as the stone wall across a high meadow seems
a necklace, felt everywhere if touched at one place,
but also matter's huge lattice, netting neither grasses
nor the bellows breath of the herd as they pass, turn, pass,
so the surface of that burning jelled and dispersed.
After these swirlings of the vast clock had risen,
after sight had sunk into the tug of its field,
a blood-rose disc condensed upward, and pinning it
in place a dot of platinum, endlessly burnt open.
There process became aperture. Under it a host, swarming,
newly fielded, might feel itself one, and two hosts meet as one,
and the turbulence in each point, seen from there
as one whiteness weaving its multitudinous
corridor, make alignment. So it seemed, for an hour.

II

It will be nothing that is not classic, delicate
and brutal, three years before its time or at most
three centuries too late; nothing that is not shadowed
on the near, impalpable white wall of the garden
by the outsized hands of last decade's costly
irrelevant timepiece. It will be just like this life,
this country place, this week of play ahead—so many
handshakes, so many bedrooms. It will be
the shoot arranged at midweek, or at some other
right time—after *pas de trois* have bubbled
into glasses and trembled at their rims. It will be
the seventh blind. The host with his entire party
circling to take their stations. Retired generals
ogling the factory owners' wives, the benign host
dreaming the calls, struts, preenings of clockwork birds
in his vast collection; behind him his mistress, well
knowing that she has no chance. Then he stops, blows
a thin brass signal, and the beaters move off
somewhere among the birches. In twenty white coats,
hats, half-filled black pouches for game,
they whack long poles against the trunks white like
themselves, stepping deliberately. Hares cower,
then dart forward. Pheasants, slanting through dry gorse,
test the perimeter. Yes, it will be just like this
shabby tattoo, hypnotic bent heads and arms,
this dead army among the leaves, while tiny eyes
and muscles go stiff, then spring away.
Suddenly the birds take to air, those tailored
men and women rise and level at the caroming
knots of fur. Each face quickly is like each other,
simpler, smoother in mist sweet with apple rot;
their arms lift in steady arcs, their wrists cradle
with slight curves the smooth stocks, and birds fall,

twisting. The hares at last pitch, spin, hurtle
furrows, while the earth around them jerks with shot.

Then quiet. The beaters stoop, retrieve. It will be
just this, no other dispersal, just these faces
becoming again themselves, and making new groups
that wend back towards the main house. Nothing if not
this scent of stubble overwhelming apples and then
yielding again to apples; nothing if not this
slight girl, lovesick, student of pre-Columbian
artifacts, who knows now how to use a gun.

So, to Bakhtin in prison, consuming backwards his own
study of Goethe as paper for his smokes, grant worded fire!
To Cellini, relisher, ravisher, and cell-sitter, give bronze.
To Constance Markievitch grant a cell's consoler beyond Yeats.
To Osip of the goldfinches, viaticum at each transit link.
To Michnik our exemplar, safety, who knows that the frightful
consequence of freedom is false transformation.
And so to Boethius, Ralegh, Gramsci, and Berrigan, grant Philosophy
as the Lady due to each solitary: alchemy's *Soror*
in the singing booth wadded shut by power yet penetrable.
In it, each made impregnable vessels and seeded them.
Grant cells that cave to an inshore pouring, that solve
to spindrift tremor, sheen of the trapped still whispering
air—eagle eats lion, grass the earth, corrodes it
to a new wax throned at the fire's heart, blown cataract
at halt in the hand's breeze then rocketing, waking mind's
marine flourescence. Give them sun through moist quartz
levering the summits, signaling in chains down the couloirs:
over shale from the sea's bed, and in the steepling
untoppled thunderhead, mosses dream of roots.
Grant them that page where night strings traffic by unshaken
rivers, lucite shafts into cool hell. Hind eats serpent,
shedding its own coat and all senility with it—
yes, grant them the king panther, who will feast

to a three-day slumber and then rise, belching breath of such
sweetness that every beast will follow it in trance
inhaling, trailing the snake's crushed head, slither
of black sun through leaves into that clearing where
they will gather in alertness: through slow heaven
and in each lifted eye, cloud rides the sea's curve.
Paper, scratchings, and their backs bend, husks from piths
rotting into dispersal, blind vegetable into soil,
mineral glint into metal, all flaking off the spin
of their horizons into the Great Bear, Centaur, and then
the Hunter—through the air's whirled involvement
procuring us meat and liquor, the rust of meteors
staining the kiss of bread, our sulfur spilling
to seas where no trace is lost: up into ventral fins
beating Anahata's rhythm, or into the cloud's body
leaning above, trailing a lace rain over shoulders
dozing among the near valleys, cold smoke on skin, brain,
to harbor there, silting portals, atlases, the new
poisons and potencies, unforeseen, all yeasting
into the *epithuma,* crud-burn in the ritual
sacrificial vessel, along the veins and hands, feeding
flame we breathe out smokelessly, odor of the kind.

Climbed a mountain, but on its peak I had not rested.

Looked down from what it afforded, yet I saw little
in a seeing way, bits had swirled enlarged in aria,
the rest had settled into the premature composure
of an animated map, a miniaturized symphonic
score page which abridged introit, false coda, and true,

while the three tubes of black metal sheathing radiance
around the pit lectern, aiming it through sedate slits,
had been removed, it was neither history nor geography
anymore, O Corsican, O Koussevitzky.

Half-light of the tundra in the long arctic day.
Through that, a clarity which telescoped a glacier
calving from its ice cliff long seconds before the thunder.
Yet I was speaking with a short man in sweaty dhoti
who prodded hardpan with the stick of his demonstration.

How they had dug, right there, and gotten down to water,
using only their own backs. Bapu was right, it would work,
and wouldn't I contribute? Presumably I was rich.
Yet looking up into the evening long as a season
the metal eye of the longspur met me from her nest,
pale eggs glowing, and I saluted them, her, the light,

the Gandhian nodding with me, to the asymptote of north
with our puffed-out breath.

III

Steadily without thrusting, wind penetrated what joy,
forceps steadily forcing wide the heart, drew open.
Such air feeds no outburst, cascade, or whelming surge:
along hair of the forearm a wheatfield submits
to a current which thrummingly that blown gold harbors.
Standing while fleeting, unreconstructible wave
brightly unbroken across mounding rock, yet
all of that sweep, were it refeatured as one stream,
would be the aware companion of stony mind. And it is,
that mind one stratum in the store of mind,
alseep in it what stirs in the grass and wakes in us.
Lying in her father's wheatfield, only eight
and so about to inherit the glasses her oldest sister
would hand on when leaving New Hampshire, Alvina
tried to disperse the weight of a dream. In it she
herself was the oncoming waves of lifetime after lifetime,

slowly working out the substance of each passage,
melting across a membrane and then being recomposed,
details fading from that sequence, but existence
the sunned wheat of an incalculable movement, as if
tiding in and out around her, washing her arms
but leaving there to carry indelibly through years
a knowledge not from books, theory from bone
and darkness, and from

harvest light of the dark.

Down a three-mile hole in the Antartic ice
hangs a photosensitive cable catching muons,
bluish spinoffs from collisions of neutrinos
which pierce everything, save for that handful
lighting up the game board of transparent matter,
under the icecap, or again in the deeps off Hawaii
showing up on thousand-foot strings of sensors
after their expulsion, with weird charge and nearly massless,
from the core furnaces of galaxies, spinning out
like David's pebble from his leather sling and its
black hole whirring and flattening and snatched back snug and dark.
The microphones, lasers, and the sunk flotation globes
wait like the net of Indra, not the brow of Goliath,
to snare in their arrays the food of thought, Brahma's
weightless trillion-electron-volted emanations.
The team setting these in place calls itself *Amanda.*
Alvina will not have read of them either, and they'll not
have blushed to appropriate, as weather forecasters for storms,
the name of a belovèd, in this case meaning just that.
Amanda *amanda est,* Alvina *ist auch sehr geliebt,*
the one seeks being, the other is being's lens,
bursts of violence in blue flashes bleeping faintly
along the cold strings, while through sleep's hot pulse
life presses its tidal mass through a girl *Loved by All,*
but masslessly.

Charged past our single handling, the amandate

alvinate *sehr geliebt* press of coming and passing
gleams blue along wiring and in nerves drifts as great weight.
Spirit shatters the body then rears it up again richly,
wrecking the house for its hoard, then with that plunder rebuilding.
Tolstoy's Levin, as he came closer to both the fiber
of what bonded him to the woman whom he chose
and the charge of the land that chose him, swung a blade
in rhythm with his serfs, the owner at last owning
in release and penetration the waves of the blown field
passing, falling to his stroke, resprouting the seasons
in green, gold, scorched, then white and sodden flashes,
over one field through generations of hands
flashing there also, wiping the brow, gone.

A story
from epic aims the incalculable charge of Arjuna
through the Amazonian arms of Chitra in one blue sputter,
with oscillations of identity: our tidal way.
The archer was his skill, his name, but unfulfilled.
Chitra had mastered the bow because her royal father,
twisting the gods to their vow of a male, bent her so.
Unmatched in her region was the bow-woman of Manipur.
Yet the matchless came there: Chitra saw Arjuna,
loved him, and despaired of herself. Blue light
cut at her soul and severed her grip on the sprung bow.
The gods gave her brief allure, it faded, but Arjuna,
having seen and held both, affirmed her: *I am fulfilled!*
He goes and comes. Let me give him Levin's dream.
Neither gold, rust, nor hair's yellow that abrupt sea before us,
stabbed by lightning in your eyes, crowding the porch in mine,
waist-high, all the wind's thing, smelling of salt aired and sifted
and the granary's bleached floor, you in one sleep, I another.
This showing stopped in a breath, in a gather of the blade
arcing before the legs, body counterweighting
steel we had never used with strength before but swung now

in long strokes. And the hands were both ours or no one's.
That was the first day. Now that it has passed, I see
further into the weave and two wheatfields spreading,
one packed in moonlight where a hunched sweating mower
labors in silver, laying his ghost swathes down alone,
faithful to something hidden, disturbingly faithful, for
he fails to see the village gather in a long file and go
into the church, and does not hear their faint chanting.
Gazing along his acre I feel the grain in fingers
rise and the long cells arch and lock, and feel the dead
uneasy in the wakeful earth. It is then
that the other field floods in, daylight in blown waves
and you beside me above me the mineral sweetly bitter
heaviness inching under as we shear and wade,
strive together and go down, but we are not left
unfulfilled, we are not separated in the swathe,
neither rust nor hair's yellow lost there nor even
our granary's floor, you in one waking, I another.

IV

The oily bronze of a fresh monument to the fallen
heaved and fell, mid-Atlantic restless in the moon.
Mind afloat there, I came unmoored. But my guide
swimming to my left shoulder gripped it gently,
and with that holding came overhead the midday sea
collecting to a focus, light-hammered limiting sky,
and then below at noon, the same workings, surface
hinting everywhere at movement while holding fast
in the mounded diaphane of our orb flowing away.
In the oiled jade around me once more suddenly
glimmered heavy glidings of cloud and patchy azure.
Peering into these I made out the encrusted
Venices of achievement slowly subsiding, and pastels

of St. Petersburg in June's nightlong-lit canals,
stalagmites of Manhattan piercing a ferry's wake,
bar of bridgeshadow unbending in the tiderace
at Golden Gate near the fault named for Christ's Andrew,
and as if at the end of voyaging, the fathomless
face of the ice continent shining with storm runoff.
But now you shall hear them, he said. And while I still saw
that panorama, detonations, muted to the rollings
of tympani in Neilsen's *Inextinguishable*
and Berg's climb, after silence, from drums to the peaks,
not from our wars but past them, unfolded and mixed
then shattered. Sea-cove channels being widened by engineers
exploded across Piazza San Marco and Hong Kong.
Bluff tankers bulled along unsullied littorals.
Humpback whales, swerving, shook with tremors then headed
repeatedly inshore, shunning the poles of helpers,
stranding themselves. The deep din narrowed to a hum.
Foam, fading, but not the froth of the seaborne empires.
Cleansings, it was, of a sweptwing porous shape
by the ammoniac hissings of subacqueous peace.
Its measure indistinct, minute or colossal, there hung
the bony sac of a whale's inner ear from fluted
verticals of coral, that ensemble counterweighted
by a massive lava spurt. With blood and yellowish
damage rinsed clean, this bascule bridge of hearing swung clear.
This, twisted within, had steered the great gray awry.
Its bulbs and coruscations flared capital without column.
The date-palm upward soarings of Karnak, the Corinthian
emanation from a god's porch, lay nascent here.
Part womb, part bricolage, seed of abstract angel.
The hum by then had become pervasive, interior
and placeless. That ear, now a gong, hung still while the whole sang.
Around it grew a similar shape: on the headland
at Samothrace, shattered also and cleansed, leaned that
figurehead, veed wings of the costly hybrid, *Victory.*

As a priest at baptism over the font, into veils
of lingering incense, lifts the unaware gowned infant
in triumph at the axis of houseling through time,
and invokes death and rebirth over the bright bud
whose upper seam, still open to the press of sound,
wobbles under the dome at the crossing, tympanelle,
so the lift of the bleached ear's grid before me
brought with its elevation torsion from below,
across the entire spread of ocean, the shelving
beaches and citied winking deltas, up through land:
Into my end you now have been ushered, children,
into my rising initiated, brash babes.
Into estuaries past unguents of the mills, into the stream
where Dalai Lama pours powders of the stripped mandala.

To him the six-and-thirtieth of those thirty-six just Jews
unknown and unknowing whose lives are what save us
in the legend, and to the hidden Muslim aware
of Mohammed who was aware too of him hidden away,
hearing is a special vocation. They have already heard
and forgotten, their job so preoccupying them
with its detail work, its piecework, its weight,
that they need no second announcement. That would be absurd,
the first one no longer within hearing and the next,
as a next, inconceivable. But the hum, that they hear.
Like the disoriented whales, but unlike them
in being exactly and anonymously aimed home,
they respond by moving and move by keeping still.
Not to them the voice at death as to Abraham,
saying, *Old one, go ride your space as a shell*
lobbed into the apex of its trajectory,
level into that zone preponderant of the quiet air
where weight and upthrust poise in the pressed ply of achievement—
graze that boundary and go, seeking the resonance
of your own caliber down the warehouse of winds.

Mountain spring and bantam heart,
rock trembling in calm underjets,
smoked gold rocking
in day's diamond, death
not holding it, O solidity
ungraspable, swirled in
bone-numbing flow.
But *Salve:* it is evening.
Closed on itself, the eye
spins its slow fire, the highway
hums like a rubbed string.

I have cast my lot
with the arrowmakers
who feel themselves at last known,
past the erratic, the undone,
by sky, by flint,
by tree and ground, and who
  stand to release.

V

Heel slithers, hunting, and the hand widens:
go farther, where smoke beads to bright mosses
slickering your foothold near a drowned lost cup.
Flesh of that sound roars *Enter* and wind eases the column
back in towards the wall: messengers, turbulence
crowding the edge above, chanting the weight of days,
the thousand works and worlds we are not. No young men
sing in this tall cave, chip at stone, no young women
brow behind brow in spray shadow model for them,
the cliff wrinkles sheen as from scar tissue. Who then
has climbed with the moss's foot, or fed with the ouzel?
Winging into the current, slope of swift water

swept off his glossy crown in a clear shell, sung crystal—
sensuality fears death but has warm ears, craves
this tiny thunder. Who has fed with the ouzel?
One listens for a long time to the torn column—
it is a sound whitening past memory
and one believes that sound—but with no column there,
nor the light weaving it, nor even the you listening:
the sound only, high flume off a dry ledge
cascading to the cloudy floor of stone. The way
through primal tone leads to strange seeing, *animula.*
What holds our eyes is the combustion, and what sears
the personal heart is heat enough, yet neither
of those long agencies itself frames the furnace,
nor alone rewards the speculation surviving
in mirrors of the molten, where the mean dances, unstill.
What stands from them, O little one, whole in its form?
Up, as the lighthouse top, swiveling, swells white,
or a wave sheens taller thinner shearing in fire,
as if wax might clarify down to the candle's base
and string's abyssal yoke in a companioning elsewhere,
matter revealing its other temperature as abruptly
as Tolstoy from dinner table and shared bedsheet
broke for the monastery, then back to that branch-line station
where the fire raked him and he lay guttering with the odd gleam
of the soul climbing along the snuffed wick to flame up
over there, among the unerring novae: flash: darkness.

In the globe thinning out, in the round slipping, a great
heat moves towards light, cooperation with which
is life, resistance to which is descent
compacting to the icy density of betrayal.
As mist, though airy, freezes in twists around a cataract.
An allegory of the yoga which conquers fear
in the face of this is not complicated. A couple,
no more harmonic than we in our own tries at the state,

yet practicing the scales more than sporadically. That yoke.
Under it they take a walk. They are on a trip,
bless them, and it is after dinner, and she is suddenly
aware of the woods trail as of the unnumbered pasts.
He has to take her hand. It is like a sentimental
photograph, if you will, of children, yet it's the world.
Writers of midrash record a glimpse of the feast
still to be set before the assembled universes
of indomitable appearance—terribly what they seem,
yet being something other—and the unseen God.
They write that the flesh of both Leviathan and Behemoth,
Devourer and Crusher, breath held till it burns, flesh's fire,
will be served to the ones who have come through, and their Source.
Death a morsel to more than life, pain to peace.
This, like the gulf of air around a hiker's head,
scents brain, tints vision, yet flees all their range
while staying as their sphere, nestling them entire.
That couple's French village rests in its valley like a tired walker
at ease with trekking through centuries: it reclines
to skin a peach and, chapel roof to boughs, taste coolness.
The pair who have chosen it found the one waitress,
the deliverer of their grilled sole, who was resentful,
and so the man grumbled. The woman smoothed this to
an occasion for recollection. That is how love sits at meat.
Their hotel room was papered with the provincial stained
prints of the ancestral pattern books. A beveled mirror,
like the facets of most human hearts, had not yet
been polished. Tarnish, silvery black, of eye and breath.
Standing with her back to him as he lay back, face reflected,
their linkage composed ordinariness of the millennial,
momentarily singular, grasplessly all-repeatable.
Starshine on a poolface, leaves blown from it,
and down the curves of that depth the paling eyes of stones.
After their meal an avenue of trees led from town
into the dark cut and stars. That is where fear

stopped her and his hand reached. Thus the scrapbook moment
enlarged to mawkish cliché for the card racks, yet it is
what they did at Eden Gate, and it will do again here.
Hers was the simplex of the toothed multiple, scaly firy,
which by grasping with gentle touch and tone he led out
among cordoning trunks and the thrown universes.
When they lay in bed, the stream fell directly under
their open window with the cleansing of rolled worlds.
Fear whitened by foam, with sound and volume of sound
rolling down fullness. The village was named for the stream,
and the stream was called *l'Abondance*. The Fullness.
And where was that? Where it always seems to hide,
at the midpoint, the between, in the two of them
extracted to the one they make elsewhere abundantly,
at crossings wearied by ancestors washed whitely down,
at the prize juncture tugged at by the Deceiver
so that his false amplitudes, his empty promise, may twist it
aside for the pair, tired walkers now lying back who nonetheless
go with *l'Abondance* in its clear plunge off and away.

VI

Registered are Augustine's offerings to the Scriptures
as he tallied his writings and withdrew over the Psalms
into his bedroom, a last harbor, to weep and prepare.
David's harmonies tuned his offering to the Alone,
harmonic with the dead who had sung them, and his guests
who had fed from them, the animated band scattered.
But unrecorded, the daily offering to a whelp
wagging at the doorsill, and a cat svelte and silent.
Offerings to the Scriptures: radio script in haversack
that would damn or dirtily ennoble him, the verdict
depending on the place of doctors at his assizes,
and it would not help the judges that this certain Pound

deemed himself during his flight north from Rome
the equal of legendary refugees among the dead,
and that his despised Virgil afforded him the hubris
of porter to the Penates of a tribe yet to come.
So can hunger for justice torque the stripe of a keen man.
A host to many, even to Vivaldi revived,
became the guest of peasant and transport driver. But always
he had been seen feeding cats at night on street corners
by witnesses both fabulous and humble, and he had
set aside offerings expressly for the free agents.
Oblations: when the other first crossed the long garden,
a Shivite who had danced in the Kaiser's corps de ballet
and tried to paint his way to Munich's other shore,
he seemed actual and fabulous at once, a white beard
jutting when he called out to the cats circling him.
Muscia! Muscia! from one who had gauged anorectic
Etruscan figurines with instinct trained both by ecstasy
and the cat's tail. *Zee fake goddess? Pehrfekt. Bhut zee po,*
eet vass zatt uf a MOHdern vhooman! Therefore
with Saint Paul craned off, the column of Marcus Aurelius
was prepared for aerial bombardment with him present,
Johannes each day inching with the sun around its spiral
carved with spolia, photographing the cargo wagons
and prisoners, the podium-stiff brigadiers, and mice
on the grain sacks, his tripod a scaffold filling with sandbags.
Thus his offering to visible script in a registry
of the cast in the overbuilt center.

Herr Felbermeyer,
drill marks in the curls of your goat-footed genii
date them, but not your kneeling and crooning over paper bag
to coax cat families past their Egyptian hauteur.
Thus one completes the agenda of oblations stipulated
for the cleansing of sins from this turn of the great round.
Muscia! a scatter under the streetlamp, a whisp over cobbles.

There is no calibration at hand for the intersection
of wren's hop, feline's crawl, and dog's amble to the hand.
Nor has measure been found, save the whole itself,
for lines that inch one man out on the jammed roads north
and the other at the sunflower's pace up gunnysacks.
Should one of them not have gone, the other would not have trailed
day's curve over that corkscrew parade, the two as halves
of one tally broken across the spine of the strange
West, one tenderness, maddened and calmed in one spasm,
to which historians devote their catlike meditations,
the stalkers, the patient waiters, judicious, gazing.
To which, as the architectural, cosmic, yet disintegral
emotion it was even then—integral of split spheres
of meaning, but not of a whole spirit—the bishop
gave his gaze, lifted and dropped by it in his last weeks,
Gothic mercenaries facing off against Vandals; which tally Rome
drew to itself and released, by a law greater than Rome's.

On that high plateau the respite of a rail fence.
A Tyroler rinsed out buckets and went around his barn,
leaving a small pasture, plank wall, and propped shovel
imprinted with himself, their momentary disposer.
I waited for him though I guessed he had gone in.
A cleared space, but the eyes do not spread it, nor from
a great height take in the emerald floor of the living,
nor can it be crossed with an unbroken desire:
again I felt a hospital waiting room in free fall,
and a railway lobby across which that same plunge . . .
but then a mercy like the farmer gone away, to leave
the green brink of the deep foreground giving onto
the weathered treasury of the wall. And then
I was following midfield grasses, where they parted
over a mouse, hunched and busy. A hawk planed in,
wingshadow went towards the creature and over it
and in each of us grew larger, sharper, in the grass also

more definite and between the blades deeply slowing,
absorbing the shape still ungathered, through the soundless
wink of judgment, into the shape of the gatherer.
I have seen the height narrow to speeding yards,
tarmac streaming through the single wingjut of shadow
that straightened and firmed, ground about to claim us.
Field and floor of the living

that does not belong to us.

Inmost embrace, Shakti couched by Shiva, joins forms
not always to our sight those of clasp, ecstasy,
connubial exchange, but also of the hidden.
Pound celebrated coitus as gnosis but hung his head
sitting slumped at the center of Arles's amphitheater,
having wandered in the dank souterrain and come out
blank into the oval before a blue immortal
meditating on that blooded sand, vortices of it
funneling through his third eye and whirling off.
A devotee of Shiva, Johannes had no need
to climb as initiate to arenas of eroded review.
Though he pampered the cats, Johannes favored the mouse
impartially, knowing what actuality poses
and contemplation requires. Sits erect in me timing
the master breath.

VII

Hoplite Sokrates proposed the choices of nonviolence,
subtle misnomer, and subsistence living without wars.
He wanted to see rituals and games at their first performance,
that is, witness, behold, *theorize:* pierce and pass through.
Evidence for his having done so is his wide-eyed
entrance into death while paying dawn's debt to the Healer.
It is easy to become possessed by the heady partials
of these integrals, serve them, and, aiming, miss badly.

Thus down paving stones night-wet, a man bisects Arles
aiming at the arena, his mind a retracted wick,
his feet seeking arches leading to the lower seats.
Not the running of the bulls, that solar *ritus,*
but a ghost spectacle, woven from day over day
set within the stones' round, eye's oval theory.
Time and the not-in-time: these murders for these reasons
printing the warm dust, erased in the hot focus,
spun in a grit of circlings laid to rest under the moon.
Nonviolence is a misnomer because it is privative.
The user, knowing what he has in his hands, steps back
into, away from, and over himself, praying for strength.
The missed aim is a subtle misapprehension
of the misnomer, as if words were cones of swirled sand
charged by the overeager hand, and the nibs of those cones
were thrust down into action with no sense of its mystery.
As if a hillside of humanity were turned over
and all that spirit were poured through one point.
Have you heard, Abraham, what I told you, what
your tribe will encounter and endure in the last days?
The trouble was that Abraham had heard. The grace was
that his heart did the hearing and so too the enduring.
The feline maketh no pact with porridge, but humankind
seeks bond with the shattering hand within and above and
anteriorly beyond, trying to see, to save.

A bronze bell is the hand's hardness around held sound.
The Inupiaq elder Igruk lived out that equation.
In camp on pack ice off the coast, he lay in their tent
on caribou skins, eyes closed, the other men talking.
Sitting up, he interrupted: *Whale coming, maybe close!*
They ran out to the opening where the huge curve rose
and blow vapor bannered the air while they harpooned him.
Igruk explained, *There was a ringing inside my ears.*
Even our night's wardress is still oscillating from

the impact eight centuries ago seen by five monks
at Canterbury. *New Moon, the upper horn splitting in fire,*
a torch spewing coals and sparks, while the whole body
writhed in agony. The damping is still readable by lasers.
Igruk and those sensors, coherent mind and light,
couched in caribou fur and a greased bakelite mount,
maintain awarenesses closely cousined on our scale,
neighboring a hunter's feelings, who portrayed
the character of the Canada Goose. *You feel it, she's gentle.*
Even if she could knock you down, she wouldn't do it.
Her frequency oscillation came to his heart clear
as a bell, as we mumble usually without considering.
All of these registers of deeds, attuned accountants,
tell us something about young Mohandas Gandhi
set down on the railway platform.

It was Maritzburg
in Natal, high in the mountains on a cold night.
Bags and coat went off with the train; he was thrown out
because he would not yield his first-class compartment,
ticket valid, purchased by his Muslim employer.
No one else was there. There were no lights.
Half-frozen, he resonated with fury. His thought
was for more than his own humiliation, it was
a gonglike thinking, with it he saw Leviathan
breach and moons burn, and the sound spread along his years
from Krishna's love song for the one *neither shaking the world*
nor shaken by it, alike in heat and cold, pleasure and pain.
It was to be a fundamentalist, a reader
of the *Gita* deaf to overtones, who would slay Gandhi.
Gandhi knew that he would be slain. Felled, he blessed;
blessing, he sustained the bell note of his warriorship.
What he was after, he said, was not to be attained,
it was always present, *Ahimsa* the goose's sound.
Or the goose character, to be uncovered: love in action.
And a woman could uncover it better than a man.

I am Kasturbai, Mohandas made me,
and Mohandas was made with me. It was her dignity
in their battles which shamed him, made him see, and expand.
Through years, after his hotwater lemonjuice and honey, she'd
follow in his steps to evening prayer and the singing.
Take the seventh step, that we may ever live as friends,
he'd said at their wedding ceremony, they were both twelve,
each of them placing a sweetened wheat cake within
the other's mouth. *I will follow close behind you always.*
But she also led. *I am Kasturbai.*

VIII

Just as an advertising floater trails its tow plane
through a blue gap, its red nylon netting rippling,
so the proposal to turn fire into cooling streamsides
followed the smiling engine of his teeth, its deceit
awash in the tailrace. He spoke in the first room
of *The Exhibition,* pleased with having mounted vestiges
of literary exiles and prison writers in neat cubes.
There were no other visitors, but the Adversary
addressed me as if I were worth a mob's weight in souls.
As spilled oil spreads fake rainbows, tie-dyed bannerings
of earth's carboniferous promise, across the flows
in parking lots, garage-floor grease, and shore eddies,
so his words and presence together effused themselves
in a chord unresolvable, a wavering harmonic.
I got out of there, turning to Carlo Levi's bare chamber
at Eboli, oil paints and a battered Dante spread flat.
But whispers penetrated. Then a Sarajevo cellar
with unfinished meal and open book. There, voice-overs,
as also through that cell near the Vatican: Gramsci's.
Finally a room with the chute denied Simone Weil
for a drop into France, and notebooks in which Father Merton would have

gone farther, rancors clarifying—both in wind from a wall angle
that held silk and paper unmoving, breath of familiar
cacophony, familiarly bodiless, *bhōhū.*
So Master of Ceremonies resonated through the walls,
another peculiar arrangement between the tribal deity
and his District Attorney, dispensing with plagues and boils
to flood the facts in the case, and their keepers, with our noise.
The fire he would play with? The heat of that temptation
which met the Rabbi of Nazareth: *Your case is special.*
I escaped by lowering myself from a window ledge
into the street, air chilling my sweat. The dead cannot
be wholly safe when the wind rolling their words is not.
I crossed into Trastevere. The first stroller
was hugely, unmistakably, Fellini with broad hat and scarf.
Behind him were GIs with vaguely Asiatic faces.
He stopped to give them assignments, each a camera,
each a little notepad; they were scouting for him
on foot, he headed for the orange city bus.
I had heard about the files he kept for casting,
photos and brief specifics, phone numbers, and then
the others with official stamps, those of criminals.
He got off the bus one block down and hopped a tram.
I stopped a soldier. They were Navajos, a unit
of Code Talkers from Iwo Jima, Guam, and Saipan.
Still young. When Iwo Jima was taken they broadcast,
Mouse Turkey Sheep Uncle Ram Ice Bear Ant
Cat Horse Intestines: Naastosi Thanzie Dibeh Shidu
Dahnestsa Tkin Shush Wollachee Moasi Lin Achi.
They were wired to their new boss with transistors.
One told me that Fellini was the only person
since they had died who believed their story of the trek
up through the Four Worlds, and how beaches
littered with dead soldiers polluted them, and how they
could forget those faces only by scanning faces in streets
until some resemblance washed the imprint away. Thus

their current utility to *il gran Federico.*
Their first catches that day were non-Italian, ramrod
Freya Stark walking with Harriet Livermore, she last heard of
(my source is the gentle Whittier) wandering in Syria
with Arabs who treated her as a holy madwoman.
Fellini ran up. Miss Stark described her project for a secret
itinerary through Venice. He bit: the Fifth World.

When mist
thickens a moonlit field and far trees, then clears as cold air
supervenes, the dark scene for a moment goes crystalline,
photonegative of the prior actuality,
a brightness to our eyes ordinarily obscured.
Eleanor Clark poked her young head up into the Fifth World
in Mexico, casually looking up Trotsky with her
formal letter. She had been drilled in convent-school French,
while the exile needed a filter for his elixir. Dominican
Sisters to Trotsky, Russian frost through Racine's, to American.
Teresa of Avila was more like Trotsky than Miss Clark,
since she had the language but her male monastic
superiors and confessors, inferiors in the Life,
edited from her discourse the spiky singularities.
Tree against the dark hung with illumination,
ice of a new clarity, being pruned, made readable.
The Fifth World follows on graces, desert deprivations,
then the solidity of the sustained branch untouched.
In the quiet blackness of a night lit with stars
you see earth's roots beneath and you hold the limits
of the cosmos. Yours, too, are the arkhē and
the approaching teleutē. Before one receives such assurance,
there is the desert fluid in its own way, Habakkuk's:
The abyss gave voice to itself, heaving up its fantasies.
Therewith the third woman who entered the Fifth World,
a returnee to Russia for reasons of bond and blood,
Marina Tsvetaeva, trailing her daughter to the slaughterhouse—

but even so deer re-enter the forest of proportions
whose misted ratios rest on no stones. Hers was the darkness:
coming to Elabuga, a populated desolation,
she went on to Chistopol, beyond her last defenses.
So for her the Fifth World requires a mercifully
secret itinerary, peregrinatio
not through Venice but, say, the Poland of Switzerland,
to Urnaesch on thirteen January, the old New Year,
where the Tree Spirits and the Cow Maidens serenade
each householder. Her, too, they would encircle, and, from
their yodels' crystalline steam, she would know: *I am home.*

IX

Reims on a cold morning in January, the mist
laced with convalescence, yet also the toughness
of maintenance and harvest in the Champagne.
I had finished coffee and roll in the main square's café
and was leaving the men's room when, surging
against the door as I pushed it out, a burly drunk,
convinced that it should swing inward, and cursing
me as his personal enemy, thrust me back and rammed
the door against its frame, calling for a chair
with which to smash it in. Two men extracted me
and gruffly inserted him, returning with disgust
to their interrupted vigil over croissants and brew.
Across the square I entered the roughly cut jewel
of the cathedral. Banners with faded colors
from Joan's victories draped chapels near the apse.
Under that glass without its irrevocable queens,
misty luminosity, though not from the muffled sun.
Then they came, processing from behind the flags,
a file of men, the central one shrouded in gray
with a faint ring of blood over his sheeted head

where a crown would have fitted, which in fact
he carried in front of him, his arms through slits in the fabric.
Before him walked a guard of three, the focal one
lifting high a Hindu dagger. I recognized
the pattern, ritually designated for the murder
of the precious *moi,* Sir President, Sir Chairman,
sinuous snakings up the hilt among brass glintings.
And then I recognized the sleeves of the shrouded man
as those of my own shirt. His knobbly knuckles were mine.
All went down the left aisle and out to the square
before I found it possible to move, following them
out into the long *place* once more quite empty.
Ceiling bulbs in the café, the pair of gruff workers,
miniaturized but reconfirmed things: this was actual.
The Maid of Orleans in wet equestrian metal, sword raked
skyward, congealed vapor from the moment and dripped.
I turned back to the portals and hunkered alongside
the west wall, feeling the air pulling and changing,
fragrant.

The scent of freshly mown barley in warm wind.
Back of the apse, not the profiles of housefronts across
the cathedral close, but a field under swift low cloud
broken here and there by sun, currents of scent
easing the skin, relaxing my clenched back and face.
With his back towards me, face intent on the breaking
surf of light, Edwin Muir stood in a Czech raincoat,
hands deep in its pockets, hat low over his eyes,
leaning gently into the strengthening draft of humid
surgings from luminous grass and bright scud.
There was no question of greeting him. The tears
down his face, the joy settling there, a hint of cold
in his frame being dissolved in a zone that seemed placeless—
with him who catalogued all the unmapped places—
unless it was the unbuilt allotments of paradise.
He was the brother never met, the father unfound,

met and found in a postwar Czech slicker with collar up.
It was not a ladder before him, yet presences
drew his longing gaze; it was not the gate
demarcated and swinging, it was the wide embrace
of a strength mated to his hunched persistent one, the Friend's,
as prelude, a mixed draft, affliction turning kindly.
If women giving birth cry for the wind of the Friend,
do they not feel Him in and behind it?

The young woman
from Czechoslovakia trying to master English, so to teach German,
met with me over *Lord of the Flies* and *Animal Farm.*
Eva had the peasant woman's build. Her father had farmed,
then was drafted into factory work after the takeover
instead of being shot. She was their only child.
This Orwell story, it is not just story to me,
this animals say to me things we feel from inside
and outside. One of my other jobs sat me at the desk
of the Nordamerika Bibliothek on flake-drifted afternoons.
Yes, I would have preferred not to, but Bartleby starved.
An American retiree collecting his week's novels
cheerfully made small talk. When I asked him about
his story, he finessed like a writer. *Oh it is*
so much nicer now, though sometimes I miss all
the excitement. . . . White hair over a whisky ad's
ruddy wellness and tailored fabric, this was the former
Chief Information Officer for U.S. Forces, Saigon.
Switzerland is a checkpoint, Hailie Selassie's gold
in its subsurface vaults and flocks of economic migration
threading the currents of its passes, papers in order.
So long, Colonel! Eva they have

excluded, so I hope to
meet her someday when her full-boned face emerges
from mist into that warm wind and she recognizes
Kafka's translator and Orkney-born tallier of the Greeks

by his Czech raincoat, and they can stand with each other
in that middle world I stumbled into back of the apse,
grassy shelf near the Meeting Place of the Two Seas,
where grass is *viriditas* becoming more than itself,
and Eva is the German teacher at last, her family's
redeemer to the satisfactory degree, freeing her
for that other idea of her nature which grows real there,
the waters of this place swirling into the warm currents
of the other place. Muir will have found Willa,
who after all found him, and they will speak with Eva
in the tongue of their meeting point, gothic uncanny Franz.
And the twa shall be ain, they'll have put by any need for speaking.
And my double will shake off his gray shroud, the phantom
of what I had been greeting the unknown that I am.

X

Which others see and know. But not in the sense
of clearing out all compromise, removing evasion,
so that the remnant be a core and the core whole.
As if that residue, quiet, wishing to come
to adamantine focus, were to have been seared
by the blast at Nagasaki like that bronze statue
of the founder of one school of Buddhism, yet stood
as he did, unmelted, though he stands now in New York
facing the Hudson, as if blown there. But he stands.
Such a thing, in its simplicity: the erect posture.
By students of animal form, and by chiropractors,
queried and inventoried and savingly pummeled,
but in the battles fought inwardly by Egyptian
practitioners of the Redeemer's gnosis, reached as
the firmest grade of effort: to stand was to attain.
Prophets old and newfangled, slain in the spirit, prefer
with our cult recruits in their suits and ties to fall flat.

Plotinus demurs: *The soul is filled full and stands at rest,*
stasa ariston. In the *Phaedrus* Sokrates stood
attentively through one day and night. The first monks
and nuns stretched it to weeks. Seneca then Gregory
chose out this figure, and Gregory of Nyssa has Moses
run while at rest, motionless while roaming at large
through limitless space.

In the Syrian gospel
the talisman we are to carry into death is an answer
to the question, *What is the sign in you of your maker?*
We are to say, *It is movement and repose.* The sharpest
surveyor of standing stones in Britain and Brittany
knows them to be aligned on the stars more accurately
than we can do with theodolite, gates for the sentinels
at the Meeting Place of the Two Seas. Where Origen on the jetty
said to Plotinus, *God leaves evil unconquered,* and Plotinus
replied, *Yes. But what then? Then it gets interesting.*
In Calcutta fights flared between the religious gangs.
Gandhi staggered from a fast to the death, and stood—
and, standing in his faintness, brought them all to heel,
for a time, that is. Behind him in his stance, Kasturbai.
They took in the untouchables. But he knew that he must
see and learn more, and so rode the trains third class,
among bedrolls and trash, going to sleep standing up.
If Malraux were to cut through jungle again to prize
bas-reliefs from some temple, he and Clara would machete
a path from Elbe to Rhein, ruined Bingen to the Rhône chapels.
Collectors in a late hour with early lusts. Our A-tests
used our own sailors, our test crashes belt in fresh corpses,
and we speak of knowledge! There must stay, unfindable, one tomb—
gold women standing, uncaptured hiddens, around the canopic shrine.
For memory's most is not backreach but the oncoming field,
not scattered personal tales but a blue peak from the axis
rupturing horizons: the fountain, its dense jet holding.
The code? A transmission suspended across the broken factors,

silently yielding the massed kinds gazing out through each other
towards the mountain, where they are remembered, where each is known.
Ghost Navajo to ghost warbler and whale, and the Jewish girl's hand
thrust into perhaps yours by her mother during a roundup,
you would become what you do, there would be no questions.
Far memory is first form freshening, as mobile
as the whole throng, yet standing as did Gandhi jolted dozing
in the third-class corridor, the facts harder, his idea firmer.
Were I to climb there again through renewed May flowers,
all of this might come with me to a last post in dusk
settling among the standing ridges.

If the actual

relations that I manage lead to actualization
of the relation I can at best imagine, then
something has notched forward. Have I myself done it?
And what has become of all the Kantian categories?
Mnemosyne, be mourned no more, at that swept speck of junctures I felt
passing the severed foreleg of a mountain goat, that hoof
poised over hoof shadow. The point about the tomb is
that no one ever find it; that the jars with bowels
of that ruler rest in gilded untouchability
behind the spread arms of golden women at a stand.
That when Clara and André come to a half-buried
Romanesque campanile, they find it as overgrown,
enticing, and irremovable as the riddle
at which they hacked in the jungle of the colony.
Should there be some recognition for me up there,
sight would not find it, but feet stilled. As a child
I envisaged a doctor, a fugitive alchemist
standing at such an overlook, experimenter
with that water which no folly may contaminate
once it has grown gold and hard in the cleared will
and dissolved bitterness of the enterprise, the one
job, the travail. Unfolding of the work worked through.
Had set there in bland fantasy when I was callow,

elsewhere and green, greenly idle but still aimed.
Between that preliminary of conjunction and my
standing there, the reared serpents rimming the shrine
lift blue, red, gold, and turquoise to balance gold suns
in the intact darkness above the four intact guardians.
Not quite touching, the flats of their extended hands
and the incised panels within four corner pillars.
Their arms but half-lifted: neither prayer nor embrace
nor startle nor unfolded welcome, and yet sweeter
than all of these. O foursquare hidden, O queened cup.
When I had gotten to the summit, I stood there long into
deepening haze, looking. There was less and less to see,
that part was over, but the whole of it I felt
piercing through, as a hawk whistled near my head, unbending, to sail down.

NOTES

III

"Spirit shatters . . . ": From the *Mathnawí* of Jalálu'ddin Rūmī, I.306-7.

"A story from epic": The *Mahabharata.*

VII

"Have you heard, Abraham . . . ?": From the Jewish apocalypse, *The Testament of Abraham.*

VIII

An actual exhibit in Rome some years ago devoted to Carlo Levi's exile in Eboli (described to me by Alfred Kern) used minimalism cannily rather than diabolically.

"Mouse Turkey Sheep . . . ": As the reader already may have observed, majuscules in the

English version of the Navajo message spell out in anagram the name of the captured peak.

"In the quiet . . . ": II.13–15 of the Orphic *Hymn to Apollo.*

The source in Whittier: *Snowbound.*

IX

"Irrevocable queens": In 1861 the historian Charles Cerf wrote, describing the glass panels destroyed by bombardment in 1917: *"Rien n'a pu ébranler la solidité des panneaux, irrevocablement attachés à leur vêtement de fer, et bravant, dans leur imperturbable fermeté, toute la fureur des plus terribles orages."*

"If women giving birth . . . ": From the *Mathnawí* of Rūmī, IV.147–48.

X

"That bronze statue": Of Shinran Shonin, 1173–1262, founder of the Joda Shinshu sect.

"In the Syrian gospel": Logion 50 of *The Gospel of Thomas.*

"The untouchables": For convenience I preserve the Western usage which, as Alain Daniélou has explained, gets things precisely backward. Rather than the lowly artisan caste, it is the Brahman caste in its ritual purity that remains untouchable.

The biographers of Malraux, and Clara Malraux in her memoir, describe the young couple's abortive attempt to slice free and transport Buddhist bas-reliefs from a temple in the jungles of French Indochina.